HUMILITY RULES

J. AUGUSTINE WETTA, O.S.B.
Monk of Saint Louis Abbey

HUMILITY RULES
Saint Benedict's Twelve-Step Guide to Genuine
Self-Esteem

IGNATIUS PRESS   SAN FRANCISCO

Cover art:

Saint Benedict with Skateboard
by Jean C. Wetta

Cover design by Augustine Wetta, O.S.B.

© 2017 Ignatius Press, San Francisco
All rights reserved
ISBN 978-1-62164-149-0 (PB)
ISBN 978-1-68149-787-7 (eBook)
Library of Congress Control Number 2017932733
Printed in the United States of America ∞

For my godmother, Tina Stretch

I see the beauty of Your grace;
I contemplate its radiance,
and I reflect its light.
I am caught up in its unspeakable splendor.
I am drawn outside of myself as I think of myself.
What I am, what I have become—O what wonder!
My eyes are open, for in my own presence,
I feel such esteem, reverence, even fear,
as though I were actually standing before You.
I am bewildered, overwhelmed by this fear.
I do not know whether to sit or stand,
what to do with these arms and legs that are Yours,
for what works, what deeds I should use them,
these wondrous divine marvels.
Grant me to speak, and also to do what I say,
O my Maker, my Creator, my God!

> —Saint Symeon the New Theologian
> *Hymns* 2, 19–27

CONTENTS

INTRODUCTION

My friend (we'll call him Egbert[1] so that you don't confuse him with any real living person) suffers from profound insecurity. He is afraid that he doesn't love himself enough. He is afraid that people don't take him seriously and that he is often overlooked because he is not assertive. Egbert worries about his body and fears that people are judging him. He is stressed out, bummed out, overworked, underappreciated, and anxious. In short, he suffers from something that we often label "low self-esteem".

I would like to help Egbert, but it's hard to know where to turn for advice. And the world is full of bad advice. If my friend asks around, he's likely to hear a lot of clichés like these: "Be true to yourself", "Follow your dreams", "Learn to love yourself first", and "You can do anything so long as you put your mind to it." These platitudes might make Egbert feel better for a time, but in the end, I fear

---

[1] Saint Egbert was a seventh-century monk and missionary. Oddly, the name seems to have gone out of style, but I'm hoping it will make a comeback.

they will only result in empty narcissism and despair.

Now it happens that there is a little-known but highly effective twelve-step self-help program that folks all over the world have been using for more than fifteen hundred years. You won't hear about it on late-night infomercials or read about it in *Vogue* or *Men's Health* because it's not about beating the competition, getting rich quick, making friends, enhancing your sex appeal, or influencing people. And it doesn't have many boisterous proponents, because those who have mastered this program tend to be content just as they are. Nonetheless, those people are happy to share what they know if you ask.

The program is called "The Ladder of Humility" and it comes from a short book by Saint Benedict called simply *The Rule*. Before we get started, however, there are surely some questions you will want answered. No one in his right mind is going to take advice from a complete stranger on an issue so important and so personal as self-esteem. So allow me to introduce my friend, Saint Benedict. Also, I'll introduce myself and try to explain why Benedict's Ladder of Humility is worth your time.

⌇

Who Was Saint Benedict?

Right around the beginning of the sixth century, there lived a teenager who was bored with school. He was at the top of his class. His father was wealthy and influential. This was a smart, charismatic kid, and he seemed destined for greatness. But he hated school.

It wasn't that he had anything against learning; he just felt like he was wasting his time. He was training to go into politics, but the world seemed to be going down the tubes. There were gangs of kids armed to the teeth in the street; there were endless, bloody wars being fought all over the world; and there was a sudden influx of terrible diseases for which there were no cures. There were scandals in politics and scandals in the Church. In short, the world was a mess.

So he ran away. But he didn't join the circus or find his fortune in The Big City. Instead, he went to live in a cave on the side of a mountain. There, without all the distractions of family and school-work and social life, he figured he could focus exclusively on holiness. He was thinking specifically of Christ's words: "If you would be perfect, go, sell what you possess and . . . follow me" (Mt 19:21). He wanted to take those words literally.

Saint Benedict spent the next three years just praying. Ironically, all this praying made him famous. People started to come to him for advice. The next thing he knew, there were hundreds of guys living in the same mountains, trying to do the same thing. Folks even invented a name for them: the *monakhoi*—the "lonely men"—or, in modern English, "monks". But each monk seemed to have his own way of doing things, with the result that there was a whole lot of chaos and not a lot of prayer going on. So a bunch of them got together and came to Benedict as a group. "Teach us how to be real monks," they said.

So Saint Benedict wrote a handbook. It was chock full of great advice, from who should apologize after an argument, to how many times a day you should pray, to what you ought to do with old underwear, and whether you should sleep while wearing a knife. It was so useful, in fact, that within a hundred years, virtually every monastery in Europe adopted it. We know it today as *The Rule of*

Saint Benedict, and it is used by monasteries all over the world, from Saint Louis Abbey in Missouri to Ndanda Abbey in Tanzania to Tupazy Abbey in Paraguay to Saint Willibrord's Abbey in the Netherlands. In all, there are more than twelve hundred monasteries and twenty-five thousand Benedictines worldwide. I'm one of them.

Who Is Augustine Wetta?

I knew a monk who used to say, "Enough of me talking about me. What do *you* think of me?" For good reason, monks tend to be reluctant to sound their own praises. The core of monastic spirituality is humility, and humility is hard to square with autobiography. Still, if you are going to spend time reading what I have to say, I can understand why you might want to know a thing or two about where I come from. So here is my story:

I grew up on an island in the Gulf of Mexico. My family belonged to a wonderful parish with a brilliant and energetic pastor named Paul Chovanec. I decided I wanted to grow up and be just like him. But around thirteen, I discovered girls and changed my mind. Also about that time, my mother insisted on sending me to Theater Camp, which was where I learned to be a nerd—or at any rate perfected my natural talent. Juggling caught my imagination and turned out to be an easy way to earn a quick buck. Two years later, I started a business with my best

friend. We called ourselves "The Flying Fettuccine Brothers". For $75 an hour, we hired ourselves out as performers at birthday parties, grand openings, street festivals—you name it. We did the whole thing: bowling balls, clubs, torches, machetes, unicycles . . .

At sixteen, I decided I didn't want to be a nerd anymore and learned to surf. The whole direction of my life changed. I still juggled whenever I needed cash, and I think my peers generally agreed that I was still a nerd, but my life began to revolve around the water. I joined the swim team, tried out for the Beach Patrol, and began a slightly more serious phase of my life. On the Beach Patrol I came face to face with death—and more than once.

I was a good student and attended Rice University, where I majored in classics. I joined the rugby team and broke a bunch of bones. I also spent a semester overseas in Rome, where I studied archaeology and learned Italian. There I encountered my first Benedictine monastery. The monks turned out to be surprisingly interesting people, and I kept in touch with several of them. When I moved to Saint Louis to go to graduate school, they told me there was a monastery nearby. I dropped in for a visit and fell in love with the place. One thing led to another. I decided to spend a summer with the monks. Then I decided to leave graduate school and join Saint Louis Abbey instead.

The rest is history, as they say. I went to seminary, earned a few more degrees (two in theology at Oxford, one in English at Middlebury College), and was ordained. Now I spend my life doing what the abbot tells me. I teach high school English, classics, and theology. I coach rugby, help train new monks, and write books like this one. But most of all, I try to be holy. Which brings us to humility.

∼

Why Humility?

Everything Saint Benedict has to say flies in the face of contemporary pop culture. He is not focused on self-love, self-praise, self-aggrandizement, or self-promotion—not focused on the self at all, but on how to relate to one another and to God in light of our strengths and weaknesses. But such clarity of vision begins to develop only when you take the focus off yourself and devote yourself body and soul to a higher purpose. According to Saint Benedict, "The body and soul are like two sides of a ladder into which God has built various steps. The ladder becomes your life, and as your heart is humbled, so the Lord will lift you up to Heaven" (*Rule*, chap. 7).

Genuine self-esteem is a form of holiness, and

holiness, in Saint Benedict's eyes, is not about self-love but self-abandonment. In fact, the whole idea of holding yourself in high esteem would sound ridiculous to him. It would defeat the very purpose of the Christian life, which is to empty one's self in order to make room for God's grace. In the words of Saint Paul, God's power is "made perfect in weakness" (2 Cor 12:9). And again, in the words of Saint John the Baptist, "He must increase, but I must decrease" (Jn 3:30).

To discover God's power in our lives, we need to climb the Ladder of Humility. In the seventh chapter of his *Rule*, which is titled "On Humility", Saint Benedict outlines the twelve rungs of this ladder. They are fear of God, self-denial, obedience, perseverance, repentance, serenity, self-abasement, prudence, silence, dignity, discretion, and reverence.

Each of the following chapters of this book explains a rung, or a step, on the ladder and begins with a quote from "On Humility". Each chapter is then broken down into sections, with more quotes from the *Rule* along the way and a homework assignment. But don't worry, the assignment is graded only on how helpful it is to you, for learning how to lean on God more as you know yourself better.

～

A Note on the Translation

Wherever I quote Saint Benedict's *Rule*, which I do after each heading, I use the classic Boniface Verheyen translation. But I've made some changes to it. The *Rule* is really old, and if you are not familiar with the language and the history behind it, you can easily lose yourself in the verbiage. So my goal here is to make Saint Benedict's handbook a bit more accessible—and perhaps a little less medieval. I've modernized the language and left out the cumbersome and confusing bits. If you want to read the whole *Rule* beginning to end, I recommend the famous 1980 version translated and edited by Timothy Fry, Timothy Horner, and Imogene Baker.

∽

SAINT BENEDICT'S
LADDER OF HUMILITY

Step 1: *Be afraid*
FEAR OF GOD

Always have the fear of God before your eyes (Ps 36:2) and avoid all thoughtlessness so that you are constantly mindful of everything God has commanded.

Step 2: *Don't be true to yourself*
SELF-DENIAL

Do not be in love with your own will, but put into practice that word of the Lord which says: "I have come down from heaven not to do my own will but the will of him who sent me" (Jn 6:38).

Step 3: *Don't follow your dreams*
OBEDIENCE

For the love of God, be obedient to those in authority over you, imitating the Lord, of whom the apostle says: He became "obedient unto death" (Phil 2:8).

Step 4: *Suffer fools gladly*

PERSEVERANCE

Be patient in suffering, even when you encounter difficulties and injustice, for Scripture says: "He who endures to the end will be saved" (Mt 10:22).

Step 5: *Put your worst foot forward*

REPENTANCE

Never hide any of the evil thoughts which arise in your heart or the evils you commit in secret. Instead, reveal them to someone you trust. For Scripture says: "Commit your way to the Lord; trust in him" (Ps 37:5).

Step 6: *Be someone's doormat*

SERENITY

When ill treatment comes your way, try to accept it. Learn to be content with the lowliest and worst of everything, and in all that is demanded of you.

Step 7: *Have a poor self-image*

SELF-ABASEMENT

Believe in your heart that you are an unworthy servant of God, humbling yourself and saying with the Prophet: "I am a worm, and no man; scorned by men, and despised by the people" (Ps 22:6).

Step 8: *Think inside the box*

PRUDENCE

Only do what is lawful, and follow the example of your elders.

Step 9: *Don't speak up*

SILENCE

Only speak when you are spoken to, for Scripture says, "When words are many, transgression is not lacking" (Prov 10:19).

~

Step 10: *Laughter is not the best medicine*

DIGNITY

Do not be too quick to laugh, for it is written: "A fool raises his voice when he laughs" (Sir 21:20).

Step 11: *Be unassertive*

DISCRETION

If you must speak, do so gently, humbly, earnestly, and quietly, with few and sensible words; for it is written: "The wise man is known by the fewness of his words."

Step 12: *Keep your chin down*

REVERENCE

Wherever you go, bow your head in prayer, remembering the words of the publican: "God, be merciful to me a sinner!" (Lk 18:13).

~

FEAR OF GOD

Always have the fear of God before your eyes (Ps 36:2) and avoid all thoughtlessness so that you are constantly mindful of everything God has commanded.

You can't have self-esteem without self-respect. And because you are made in the image and likeness of God (Gen 1:27), that means you begin by respecting God. Now when the Bible talks about respecting God, the term it uses is *theosebeia*—literally, "god-fearing".

FEAR OF GOD IN THOUGHT

A monk should constantly keep in mind that all who despise God will burn in Hell for their sins, and that eternal life is prepared for those who fear Him.

—Chapter 7: Humility

Y ikes. Is this really where we are going to start? To be sure, Hell isn't the most pleasant or uplifting topic, but as a starting point, you could do worse. After all, if you are not entirely sure where you are headed, it can help to know what you want to avoid. What's more, Benedict's dreadful warning can serve as an antidote to that spiritual apathy so common among the wealthy and comfortable (and by that I mean folks like you and me). Sure, we say that God is just and all-powerful and omniscient and all that, but lately it seems we've begun to think of God not so much as a Heavenly Father but more as a heavenly grandfather—a kindly, but somewhat senile old dude who doesn't really care what the young folk are up to so long as no one gets hurt. And even if someone does get hurt, He's not likely to think about it or even remember it later.[1]

[1] C. S. Lewis wrote something similar in his book, *The Problem of Pain*. Read it. I promise it will be worth your time.

29

The stern Pantocrator they used to paint on the ceilings of ancient cathedrals—Jesus, the Judge of Nations, Lord of Lords, King of Kings enthroned over the earth—we seem to have forgotten Him too. We live in more civilized times. We prefer now to think of Jesus as more of a facilitator, or a group therapist, perhaps. But let's not forget that He is the Lord who sits at the right hand of God the Father—who will rule with "a rod of iron" and "tread out the wine press of the fury of the wrath of God the almighty" (Rev 19:15).

I'm not suggesting that it is good to be *afraid* of God—as though He were sitting up there in Heaven itching to hit the "smite" button on His computer. But then again, if God is truly good, then He must be truly just. Moreover, if our actions in this world are to have any real significance, they must have real consequences in the world to come. So yes, it's better to love God; but when you are not feeling the love, at least try to feel the fear. As the Book of Proverbs tells us, "The fear of the LORD is the beginning of wisdom" (9:10). It's not the ideal, but it's a start.

HOMEWORK: Spare the life of a bug. Bonus points if it's a mosquito.

~

FEAR OF GOD IN WORD

*Give up your own will, and take up the strong
and most excellent weapons of obedience to do
battle for Christ the Lord, the true King.*

— Prologue

was visiting a church not long ago when I noticed a boy in line for Communion wearing a
T-shirt that read, "Jesus is my homeboy."[2] I
guess I can see how that might help to break down
some barriers when it comes to rediscovering one's
dignity as a brother of Christ; but remember that
Jesus is also our King. If you don't find His divine
power a little intimidating, there's probably something wrong with you. After all, the most basic
human response to God is fear. Remember what
Peter said when he first met Jesus? "Depart from
me, for I am a sinful man, O Lord" (Lk 5:8).

When I first entered the novitiate here at Saint
Louis Abbey, my novicemaster asked me, "What
do you have to offer that would make us want to
take you?"

I told him I was smart, hard-working, and clean.
He said, "You're not ready."

---

[2] If the boy were a Spanish-speaker, his T-shirt could have re-
ferred to a particular friend named Jesús. But I doubt it.

Every day he would ask me the same question, and every day, I would think of some other admirable quality. Every day, he would tell me I wasn't ready.

Finally, after one particularly rough morning, I told him I had nothing to offer.

"Now you are ready," he said.

We shouldn't be in the habit of thinking that Jesus would be grateful for our friendship. We should love Him, but we should also be in awe of Him. His very name has all the power of the Holy Word revealed to Moses on Mount Sinai—a word so sacred that pious Jews do not dare to speak it aloud.

And of course, we should never use that name as a curse.

Don't get me wrong, our ultimate objective is to discover the perfect love that "casts out fear" (1 Jn 4:18); but be careful that you don't wind up sliding into a comfortable familiarity that drives out respect. As Blessed John Henry Newman said, "Fear and love must go together; always fear, always love, to your dying day."[3]

HOMEWORK: Let someone less competent than you tell you what to do.

∽

[3] John Henry Newman, "The Religion of the Day", *Parochial and Plain Sermons* (San Francisco: Ignatius Press, 1997) 206.

FEAR OF GOD IN DEED

Since idleness is the enemy of the soul, the brethren should be employed in manual labor at certain times. At other times, they should read spiritual books.

— Chapter 48: Work and Prayer

In his lyrical meditation on the nature of work, rock legend Todd Rundgren famously sang, "I don't wanna work. I just wanna bang on the drum all day." The irony underlying his lyrics was that in avoiding work, Rundgren wound up doing more work than he would at a regular job.[4] And so he provided us with a reflection on the nature of labor itself. Adam's work in the Garden of Eden was thrilling, painless, and endlessly fruitful, but because of his disobedience, he was condemned to earn his bread by the sweat of his brow (Gen 3:19).

Here's the catch though: Jesus worked (see Mk 6:3); so work, which was once a punishment, has become for all of us a sacred duty and a redemptive act. By virtue of this humble work, we not only

---

[4] Randy Bachman introduced a similar concept in his aptly titled song "Taking Care of Business": "I love to work at nothing all day."

bring ourselves into closer conformity with Christ, but actually help bring creation itself to perfection. We complete God's work!

Therefore, your work—whether it is a chore around the house, a homework assignment, a sports practice, or a job with an office and a paycheck— isn't just a means to an economic end. Nor is it something you need to "get over with" in time for the weekend. It is an essential part of your sanctification, a share in the divine brotherhood of Christ, and a means of discovering your true self. So the next time you are inclined to grumble about how much work you have to do, try to remember that even this is an honor because it has been redeemed by Jesus. If it was good enough for Him, it should be good enough for you. In the words of the prophet Azariah, "Take courage! Do not let your hands be weak, for your work shall be rewarded" (2 Chron 15:7).

HOMEWORK: Secretly do someone else's chores.

~

SELF-DENIAL

Do not be in love with your own will, but put into practice that word of the Lord which says: "I have come down from heaven not to do my own will but the will of him who sent me" (Jn 6:38).

What feels best for you may not be best for the people around you. For that matter, it may not be good for you either. Someone with genuine self-esteem understands that self-fulfillment is not about self-satisfaction. Thus he is willing to deny his own desires for the sake of the future, for the sake of the people around him, and for the sake of his immortal soul.

SELF-DENIAL IN THOUGHT

Sarabites[1] are the absolute worst kind of monks. Living without a shepherd, they invent their own monastery, which isn't even in the Lord's sheepfold but in their own. The gratification of their desires is their law because what they like they call holy, but what they happen to dislike they call unlawful.

—Chapter 1: The Different Kinds of Monks

rother Aidan, one of the young monks of my monastery, tells the same joke at the start of every Lent: "This Lent, I'm going to do lots of fasting, but only when I'm not hungry." His point, I think, is that all of us love the rules when they are easy to follow, but make excuses as soon as they become difficult. Saint Benedict doesn't have much patience for this kind of behavior. He utterly despises the do-it-yourselfers who make up their own rules as they go—or worse yet, follow only the rules that coincide with what they are already doing. And Jesus wasn't patient with phonies either. He reserved his very harshest

---

[1] In the early Church Sarabites were monks who lived independently, without following the authority of a superior.

41

insults for the scribes and the Pharisees. He called them hypocrites, blind guides, vipers, and white-washed tombs.

Not long ago, one of my students raised his hand and declared point-blank that there was no such thing as sin. I think he was trying to get a rise out of me, but before I could answer, the kid in front of him turned around and said, "So you are smarter than Jesus?" I couldn't have put it better myself. Unless you are truly convinced that you are holier and wiser and smarter than the combined resources of the entire Church, you might as well concede that your pastor speaks with more authority than you do.

In class a few days later, the same boy raised his hand. When I called on him, he turned around to the rest of the group and said, "I see what you guys do on the weekends. You're no better than anyone else. At least I'm true to myself." There's a part of me that has to admire a kid like this. He certainly had the courage of his convictions, and I congratulated him for that.[2] The problem was that he didn't actually know what his convictions were. After all, anyone can be true to himself. If you want to do something really courageous and admirable, try being true to someone *better* than yourself— like, say, Jesus.

HOMEWORK: Skip the next episode of your favorite television show. (You can make it up later if you must.)

~

---

[2] While in college, this student stirred up just as much trouble there as he stirred up back in high school—except that he discovered he could make much more trouble by *defending* Christian doctrine!

SELF-DENIAL IN WORD

*If an older man asks to be received into the mona-
stery, don't be too quick to accept him; if he per-
sists in his request, let him know that he must
keep the whole discipline of the Rule, and that
nothing will be relaxed in his favor.*

—Chapter 60: Older Men Who
Ask to Join the Community

hy did God make you? God made you
to know Him, to love Him, and to
serve Him in this world, and to be
happy with Him forever in Heaven. Whatever your
job is, whatever your gifts are, no matter where you
come from or where you think you are headed, this
is the purpose of your existence, and anything else
you do is just icing on the cake. You may be a cop,
a doctor, a tennis pro, or a telemarketer, but your
ultimate purpose on this earth is the same.

Benedict makes this clear from the start, especially when an older fellow decides to join the
monastery—a man who has perhaps grown accus-
tomed to a certain level of prestige and autonomy.
He may have had a distinguished career, he may
have attained power and influence in the world,
but once he sets foot in the monastery, he's just

another monk. Within these walls, "all are one in Christ Jesus" (Gal 3:28). Anything he does from now on must be accompanied by the deepest detachment, and only with the permission of the abbot. We can take from this an essential lesson about life: our dignity as human persons does not rely on our words, talents, achievements, or test scores. It doesn't even depend on our virtue.

Every evening after dinner, the monks of Saint Louis Abbey assemble in the calefactory (monkish for "living room") for about half an hour to hang out together as a family. Before I entered the monastery, I tried my hand at stand-up comedy, and I guess I still have a bit of the entertainer in me because after one of these nightly get-togethers, the abbot took me aside and said, "Brother Augustine, you have a shining star of a personality. But sometimes, lesser stars need to have a chance to shine as well." It's the nicest way I've ever been told to shut up.

The fact is we are all stars. We are all infinitely valuable because we are children of God (Gal 3:26). When we learn to acknowledge that dignity in ourselves, we won't feel like we need to prove it to others.

HOMEWORK: Let someone tell you a story you have already heard.

∿

SELF-DENIAL IN DEED

Each monk should sleep fully clothed so that he will be ready to rise in the morning as soon as the bell rings. However, he should not wear his knife to bed or he might roll over and stab himself in his sleep. Moreover, the older monks should have their rooms near those of the younger ones. Thus they may gently encourage one another on the way to morning prayer, because sleepy monks like to make excuses.

—Chapter 20: How the Monks Should Sleep

am proud to say that the Benedictines are the only religious order that has a stipulation in their rule regarding how they should handle their weapons (this goes back to the Middle Ages, when pretty much everybody carried a knife). I never get tired of quoting this passage, though I've had few occasions to obey it. I've never been at risk of stabbing myself in my sleep.

On the other hand, I do have some trouble waking up in the morning. My first ten years in the monastery, I used to roll out of bed onto the floor when I heard the bell. It hurt, but it was the only way I could keep from falling asleep again. And to be honest, even this strategy wasn't entirely

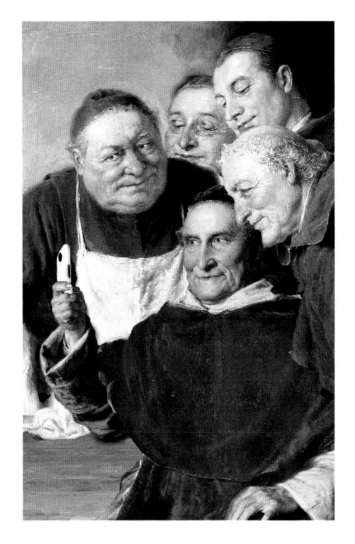

successful. I remember my novicemaster saying to me, "Brother, a monk who sleeps through his prayers is like a soldier who sleeps through his watch." That may sound dramatic, but the danger is real. We must be vigilant, for "the devil prowls around like a roaring lion, seeking someone to devour" (1 Pet 5:8). With such an enemy nearby, Christians must be ready to rise at a moment's notice to do spiritual combat. And "the weapons of our warfare are not worldly but have divine power to destroy strongholds" (2 Cor 10:4).

Moreover, it is the job of the elders to keep the young ones from getting rowdy, because if they are up all night messing around, they will be very little use at prayer the next morning. I am convinced, in fact, that fifty percent of holiness is simply getting to bed on time. No matter what sort of soldier you are, it's easier to keep watch when you are well rested.

HOMEWORK: Make sure the last thing you read tonight before going to bed is Scripture.

~

OBEDIENCE

*For the love of God, be obedient to those in au-
thority over you, imitating the Lord, of whom the
apostle says: He became "obedient unto death"
(Phil 2:8).*

Everyone has dreams, and if all of us followed all
of them, the world would collapse into chaos and
ruination. Some folks have dreams that are un-
healthy, self-defeating, reckless, stupid, or just plain
evil. So how do we know which dreams to follow?
We seek the advice of someone older and wiser
than ourselves. G.K. Chesterton once said, "We
do not really want a religion that is right where we
are right. What we want is a religion that is right
where we are wrong."[1] Obedience is what saves us
from following the wrong dreams.

---

[1] G.K. Chesterton, *The Catholic Church and Conversion* (San
Francisco: Ignatius Press, 2006), 115.

OBEDIENCE IN THOUGHT

When a monk is told to do something, he will instantly quit his own work and, leaving unfinished whatever he was doing, set about what he is told with the ready step of obedience.

— Chapter 5: Unhesitating Obedience

No one likes to be told what to do, and these days more so than in the past, people like to do their own thing. "I did it myyy waaaay," sang Frank Sinatra. Unfortunately, when you insist on doing everything your way, what usually happens is that you repeat someone else's mistakes. Every angst-ridden adolescent in the world rebels against his parents. If you want to be unique, try obeying them.[2] Better yet, try following *the* Way and not just your way. Again, this requires a healthy sense of your limitations. You have to be humble enough to admit there is someone in the world smarter than yourself.

The purest and most gracious example of obedience is Jesus' mother. When she said that earth-shattering Yes to God's angel, she couldn't possibly

[2] There are, of course, some truly bad parents in the world. If your parents are cruel or ask you to do immoral things, then you have some very hard decisions to make.

have known how gloriously her own story would end—or how much pain she would have to endure getting there. In fact, as biblical scholars are quick to point out, she had every reason to believe that her life would be short and tragic. Yet she responded to God's call with heroic obedience. In his great commentary on the *Rule*, Dom Paul Delatte calls this "supernatural docility".

"Docile", however, is not an adjective I would easily or accurately ascribe to myself—or to many of the people I like. To the modern ear, it sounds anything but heroic. Can you imagine anyone describing Batman as "docile"? Or, James Bond? Or, Superman? Yet, in the presence of God's will, what are the alternatives? So often, we find ourselves saying, "If I only knew God's will, I would do it." Well, sure. Who wouldn't? The point is to accept God's will without knowing it—to sign our lives onto a blank check. That is what is meant by Christian obedience, and it is the only legitimate source of self-confidence.

HOMEWORK: The next time you see something not done your way, leave it be if it works.

~

OBEDIENCE IN WORD

If the monks have been working in the fields or if the heat of the summer is great, lunch may have to be moved earlier. The abbot should arrange for this so that whatever the brethren do, they may do it without having good reason to complain.

— Chapter 41: Meal Times

enedict is willing to shorten the morning fast because he doesn't want to give his monks "good reason" to complain. And food is one of those things that people tend to complain about. On their way out of Egypt, the Israelites complained about not having enough to eat (Ex 16:3); and when the Lord sent them manna and quail, they complained that there wasn't enough to drink (Ex 17:2). Whenever I read that passage from Exodus, I envision God doing a facepalm of cosmic proportions and groaning, "Are you serious? After all I've done for you, you are complaining about the *food*?"

Yet, it is hard to be holy, to stay on course, when one is hungry. If you're fasting, that's one thing; if you simply don't have enough to eat, or you've been choking down the same gruel for days on end, things are likely to go south in your spiritual life.

Nevertheless, the hallmark of a really strong soul is the ability to be joyful even when the going gets tough, because a good reason doesn't make grumbling, which is a form of ingratitude, less wicked.

One might even argue that grumbling for good reason is worse than grumbling for a bad reason precisely because there is a basis for it. Justifiable grumbling is more likely to spread, less likely to stop, and far more likely to hurt someone's feelings. How often have you heard someone preface an unkind remark with something like the following: "I'm not saying anything I wouldn't tell him to his face"? Listen, pal, just because you would say it to his face doesn't mean you should say it behind his back.[3] Better, then, to abstain from all grumbling—justified and unjustified—and to pray with the psalmist, "Set a guard over my mouth, O LORD, keep watch over the door of my lips!" (Ps 141:3)

HOMEWORK: At dinner tonight, serve yourself the crunchy heel of the bread, the blackest banana, the smallest piece of pizza, or whatever looks least appetizing on the table.

∼

---

[3] I once overheard one of my students tell someone, "If you have to say something bad about me, at least make sure it isn't true."

OBEDIENCE IN DEED

The brethren must be obedient not only to the abbot, but also to one another, knowing that this path of obedience is how they will reach God.

—Chapter 71: Mutual Obedience

Monks aren't just obedient to their abbot, they are obedient to one another as well—and in particular to their elders. This goes way beyond doing what they're told and requires enormous amounts of patience.

A few years ago, I was asked to preach at my best friend's wedding. I find preaching to strangers fairly easy, because they don't know my past. But it's hard to think of anything serious to tell my friends. I did, therefore, what I always do when I'm running low on wisdom: I went looking for Father Luke. He is the founder of our community, and he has seen pretty much everything a monk can see. I found him asleep in a chair in the calefactory. "Wake up, Father," I said, "I need something wise to say at my buddy's wedding."

Father Luke opened his eyes, looked around the room for a moment, then said, "Tell him that there will come a day when he will want the window

open and she will want the window closed." Then he went back to sleep.

When it comes to living with someone, everything boils down to forgiveness. "Love is patient and kind. . . . Love bears all things, believes all things, hopes all things, and *endures* all things" (1 Cor 13:4, 7; emphasis added). So true love is more about endurance than it is about chocolates and teddy bears. We prove our love at precisely those moments when the people we love test our patience, put a strain on our kindness, and tempt us to anger. Love is truly love—and not just infatuation—when it proves itself in the crucible of suffering.

HOMEWORK: The next time someone treats you unfairly (cuts in line, plays loud music, eats something with your name on it in the fridge . . .) smile and thank God for him.

~

PERSEVERANCE

Be patient in suffering, even when you encounter difficulties and injustice, for Scripture says: "He who endures to the end will be saved" (Mt 10: 22).

In the words of Mother Teresa, "God does not require that we be successful—only that we be faithful." Fidelity in the midst of failure is called perseverance.

64

PERSEVERANCE IN THOUGHT

A monk should desire eternal life with all spiritual longing and keep the day of his death always before his eyes.

—Chapter 4: The Tools of Good Works

D o you know why monks wear black? To remind us of our death. Kind of morbid, eh? Or maybe not. If there's one remedy for grumpiness, it's this simple fact: you could be dead. The chief mark of the Christian, wrote Saint Basil "is to watch daily and hourly and to stand prepared in that state of total responsiveness pleasing to God, knowing that the Lord will come at an hour that he does not expect."[1] This vigilance is the mark of a Christian. And yet, I'll bet that very few of us, when we woke up this morning, seriously considered the possibility that the world might end today.

Now it happens that a few summers ago, I did come face-to-face with the reality of my own death. I spend a few weeks every summer in Ocean County, New Jersey, where my parents live, and I found to my delight that the surf at Seaside Heights

[1] Basil, *The Morals* 22, quoted in *Luke*, Ancient Christian Commentary on Scripture, New Testament 3, p. 214.

was really up. I also found (to my distress) that a fourteen-foot great white shark had been frequenting my favorite spot.

I went surfing anyway, because when you've only got three weeks to catch a year's worth of surf, you just have to take what you are given. I wasn't there more than five minutes when I heard someone on the beach yelling the words that every surfer hopes he will never hear: "Shark!" When I looked up, I saw about ten yards to my left a great grey fin gliding toward me through the water.[2] Laughing, crying, screaming hysterically, I paddled as fast as I could for the shore.

---

[2] If you don't believe me, you can look up "Surfing Monk Nearly Eaten by Shark" on ABCnews.com. The crucial word there is *nearly*.

Obviously I made it back in one piece. But I had two great moments of clarity during that short, frantic sprint to the beach: First, I learned that you can't paddle a surfboard without putting your hands in the water; second, I realized that while the world as a whole may not end any time soon, my own particular world could end at any moment. I also saw that many of the things that worry and distract me about this present life are of no consequence in the next.

The key to perseverance is keeping your eyes on the goal. For every Christian, that goal lies just beyond the gates of death. Our true citizenship is in the only place where we will truly feel at home: Heaven (Phil 3:20).

HOMEWORK: Spend an entire day without correcting anyone.

~

PERSEVERANCE IN WORD

Above all, there should be no grumbling—not in word, not by gesture, not for any reason whatsoever. If anyone is caught grumbling, he should be severely disciplined.

—Chapter 34: How Each Monk Should Be Treated

Sometimes, when I'm giving a tour of our monastery, I'll put this question to the guests: "What do you think is the one thing Saint Benedict absolutely forbids his monks to do?" I usually hear answers like "Kill somebody" or "Steal from the church" or "Run off with a woman." But those things don't frighten Benedict the way grumbling does.

Nothing will take the wind out of your sails like grumbling. This is Saint Benedict's pet peeve, and he mentions it eight times in the *Rule*. Twice, he begins with the emphatic *ante omnia*—"above all else". The *Rule* is a short document, and Benedict rarely repeats himself, so you know that stopping complaining before it has a chance to start must be important to him.

If you think about it, an outright fight is easier on a community than that ceaseless, cowardly, whining

gossip that comes from a grumbler who "spreads strife" and "separates close friends" (Prov 16:28). Unlike direct disobedience, grumbling makes everyone restless and angry—including the grumbler himself. "They learn to be idlers, gadding about from house to house, and not only idlers but gossips and busybodies, saying what they should not" (1 Tim 5:13).

The worst part is, there's no easy way to stop those who grumble and gossip. If someone has a problem with you, wouldn't you prefer that he come right out and tell you? But when someone goes whispering behind your back, there's no way to defend yourself without looking equally obnoxious. Saint John Chrysostom wrote, "It is better to do nothing than to do it with murmuring, for even the very thing itself is spoilt. . . . For murmuring is intolerable, most intolerable; it borders upon blasphemy. . . . It is a proof of ingratitude; the murmurer is ungrateful to God."[3]

If you want to be holy, happy, and humble, avoid grumbling *above all else*.

HOMEWORK: Keep your next opinion to yourself.

~

[3] John Chrysostom, "Homily 8", in Nicene and Post-Nicene Fathers 1, ed. Philip Schaff (Grand Rapids, Mich.: Eerdmans, 1886), 13:394, Christian Classics Ethereal Library, www.ccel.org/ccel/schaff/npnf113.iv.iii.ix.html

PERSEVERANCE IN DEED

The stability of our community is the workshop where we practice the spiritual art relentlessly day and night.

—Chapter 4: The Tools of Good Works

The last time I visited my parents at the Jersey shore, I went on a sort of pilgrimage. I use the term "pilgrimage" in the loosest possible *Webster's Dictionary* sense of "a journey to a place associated with something or someone well known". It wasn't by any stretch of the imagination a religious pilgrimage, but it was something I had been meaning to do for years. My parents live no more than a few minutes from where a popular reality show was filmed,[4] and I decided that it was a terrible shame to live so close to something so famous and not know anything about it. So I went to see it. I didn't last long. The boardwalk was, as I expected, packed with teenagers.

At the risk of fulfilling all the stereotypes of the angry, uptight old preacher, I have to say I was shocked. I mean, I grew up on a beach. I lived with

---

[4] The show featured eight twenty-somethings rooming together in a beachouse on the boardwalk.

eight rugby players in college. I was expecting noise
and rowdiness and mischief and rebellion. One of
my roommates in college had a poster that said,
"If it's too loud, you are too old." I was expecting
volume.

What I wasn't expecting was the emptiness.
These kids looked so vacant, so used. They were
tattooed and pierced and tanned to the point of
exhaustion. They seemed stupefied by excess. And
that wasn't the worst of it. The thing that really sad-
dened me was their innocence. As a teacher, I've
grown acutely sensitive to that certain way a kid
looks when he knows he's misbehaving. I know
that guilty look. These kids didn't look like that.
They didn't look guilty. They just looked tired.
And it was this more than anything that convinced

me that they truly did not know any better. That was the saddest part of the whole experience: the sudden realization that no one had ever suggested to them that there might be an alternative.

Your job is to be that alternative. You must go out and be a witness of peace and stability to a culture that has lost its balance—to show others how to fill that emptiness. And you can't do this by shouting at them. That will just add to the noise. You need only to *be* there, as "children of God without blemish in the midst of a crooked and perverse generation" (Phil 2:15), living witnesses to the power of quiet perseverance.

HOMEWORK: Smile at someone who doesn't look like they're going to smile back.

～

REPENTANCE

*Never hide any of the evil thoughts which arise
in your heart or the evils you commit in secret.
Instead, reveal them to someone you trust. For
Scripture says: "Commit your way to the Lord;
trust in him" (Ps 37:5).*

Perseverance is valuable only if you are doing something good. Otherwise, what you need is repentance, because if what you are doing is bad or stupid,
you need to be willing to quit—or at least to ask
for help.

REPENTANCE IN THOUGHT

The monk should confess his sins to God daily in prayer with sighs and tears, and resolve to amend them for the future. Later, he should reveal those thoughts to a spiritual father.

— Chapter 4: The Tools of Good Works

enedict wants his monks to feel truly sorry for their sins, but he also knows from experience that human beings have a tendency to go to extremes. In the spiritual life, this can be especially dangerous because so much more is at stake, and if the devil can't get us to do the wrong thing, he'll try to get us to do the right thing in the wrong way. "There is a way which seems right to a man," says the Book of Proverbs, "but its end is the way to death" (14:12). This is why the "spiritual father" is so important. He can help put things in perspective.

The day I entered Saint Louis Abbey as a postulant, I swore to myself that I would never again have a lustful thought. That resolution lasted all of fifteen minutes, so I decided to postpone it until my novitiate. When that time came, however, I found that I was still bothered by the same lustful

thoughts. While reading a biography of Saint Benedict, I learned that when he was tempted, he threw himself into a rose bush; so I said to myself, if Saint Benedict can do it, so can I. I went out into the garden behind the monastery and jumped right in.

Unfortunately, I had failed to take into account three important differences between Saint Benedict and me: First, Saint Benedict jumped into a *wild* rose bush, which has considerably smaller thorns than the cultivated variety; second, Saint Benedict was naked when he did it, so he didn't get his clothes tangled up; and third, Saint Benedict was a saint. Rolling around in a rose bush might be a good thing for a saint to do, but for the rest of us, it's kind of dumb. I got stuck in that rose bush and spent a very uncomfortable hour and a half trying to get out—then another awkward twenty minutes or so explaining myself to the monk who found me there.

It may be worth adding that, though stupid, the rose bush did work. Practically speaking, there was no way I could give in to temptation while I was stuck in the garden. But if I threw myself into a rose bush every time I was tempted, I might as well become the gardener. Problem is, I would make a lousy gardener.

Once the monk finished laughing, he suggested that, in the future, I would do well to check with the abbot before attempting any further feats of asceticism. Of course, I ignored that advice and wound up giving myself ulcers by fasting too much. But that's another story.

HOMEWORK: Take the blame for something you didn't do. (There will be an opportunity.)

～

REPENTANCE IN WORD

If anyone makes a serious mistake or misbehaves in some other way, let him tell a spiritual father who knows how to heal his own wounds, and not make public the faults of others.

—Chapter 46: How to Fail

In my monastery, we share a laundry room. We have an iron that everyone uses. Of course, we are always breaking it and buying replacements. But one time, I picked it up and it fell to pieces in my hands—the handle fell off, the wires fell out, and the water in the steam compartment poured out on the floor. Apparently, the last monk to use it had broken it, but instead of owning up, he had pieced the darn iron back together and left it balanced on the ironing board for the next person to break. I spent the rest of the day angry.[1]

Whether it's a broken iron or a broken promise, all sin has an effect on the broader community—even private sin, because, as they say, no man is an

[1] Turns out, the culprit was one of the old monks. He had spent all day piecing the iron back together with what he thought was superglue. In fact, he was using eye drops.

island. The whole world shifts slightly closer to the void every time we act contrary to God's will. Our actions have real consequences. "For nothing is hidden that shall not be made manifest, nor anything secret that shall not be known and come to light" (Lk 8:17).

Different religions call this by different names: "karma", "tao", "the law of consequences" . . . Even science has a name for it—Newton's Third Law: "For every action, there is an equal and opposite reaction." So instead of letting the world fall to pieces, set it right again by repenting of your sins. After all, much more is on the line than your own soul.

Granted, apologizing to God is a little more complicated than apologizing to another person, because we have such a tendency to deceive ourselves. This is why Saint Benedict insists that we confess our sins aloud to another person. He gets this straight from Scripture, of course. "Confess your sins to one another," wrote Saint James, "and pray for one another, that you may be healed. The prayer of a righteous man has great power in its effects" (Jas 5:16). Admittedly, this is a lot to ask, and you have to find a very trustworthy person; but if you want to have an accurate, honest sense of yourself, then confession is necessary. Whether it is a big sin or a little sin, the important thing is that you come right out and talk about it, because there's nothing worse for a spiritual wound than to cover it up. "Sunlight," wrote Louis Brandeis, "is said to be the best of disinfectants."[2]

HOMEWORK: Fix something you didn't break or clean something you didn't dirty.

∼

---

[2] Louis Brandeis, *Other People's Money and How the Bankers Use It* (New York: Frederick A. Stokes, 1914) https://archive.org/details/otherpeoplesmone00bran.

REPENTANCE IN DEED

If a brother notices that one of his elders is angry, let him without delay cast himself down on the ground at his feet and beg for a blessing.

— Chapter 71: Mutual Obedience

A real Christian community needs all of its members to look out for one another. Therefore, the moment a monk senses that he has done the opposite—inspired some anger or anxiety in his brother—he stops what he's doing and fixes it.

Here again, Saint Benedict demands instant and unhesitating action. A good monk will try to make humility his special virtue, so that there is no room for excuses or finger-pointing. He doesn't stop to ask himself if he's really in the wrong. The moment he perceives that his actions have caused a problem, he throws himself on the floor and begs a blessing. Notice that, technically speaking, he isn't asking for forgiveness, at least not at first. It may be that he wasn't at fault, so instead of asking forgiveness, he asks for a favor. And notice that he gets down on the floor to do it. The physical part is essential, and partly because it's so easy to do. He doesn't have to put on a sad face or try to look like he means

it. By making himself physically smaller than his brother, he restores some of the dignity he took away when he provoked him. And he can do all this while he is still hopping mad.

Again, he doesn't wait to figure out whether he feels sorry. "Do not let the sun go down on your anger," writes Saint Paul (Eph 4:26). So the monk doesn't wait to decide whether he is really at fault. He just does what the *Rule* tells him. This may sound insincere, but think about it: If people apologized only on those occasions when they knew they were wrong, apologies would be very rare indeed. After all, who ever gets in an argument knowing that they are mistaken?

Never water down an apology with an excuse.

If you've done wrong, own up to it. In fact, even if you haven't done wrong, find a way to make amends. Throw yourself on the floor and beg for a blessing. Then let the whole thing go.

HOMEWORK: Make no excuses the next time you are reprimanded.

～

SERENITY

When ill treatment comes your way, try to accept it. Learn to be content with the lowliest and worst of everything, and in all that is demanded of you.

If you are upset when someone insults you, don't put the blame on him. You were a pile of dry leaves; he was just the breeze that blew you over.[1] Granted, you do not have to be *everyone's* doormat, but remember when you are insulted that to some extent, you probably had it coming. What's more, every insult is an opportunity to practice the art of serenity.

---

[1] I didn't think up this metaphor on my own. I stole it from the spiritual conferences of Abba Dorotheos of Gaza, one of the very first monks. Look him up. He's awesome.

SERENITY IN THOUGHT

*The abbot must never be excitable, anxious,
obstinate, jealous, or suspicious. Such a person
is never at rest.*

—Chapter 64: How to Elect an Abbot

My first encounter with monastic serenity occurred during my novitiate. Saint Louis is located at the intersection of three rivers, and it is prone to violent storms. The locals call them "gully washers". Fantastic flashes of lightning accompany ear-splitting bursts of thunder, and the wind rips trees right out of the ground. The rain comes down so hard, it leaves bruises. One spring afternoon, in the middle of one of these storms, the electricity went out in the monastery and my novice-master was stuck in the elevator for three and a half hours.

For *three and a half hours*, he sat in the pitch dark waiting for the community to notice he was missing. And when we did, he emerged from the elevator . . . beaming. No one even knew he was in there because he never called for help. When I asked him why he wasn't upset, he seemed surprised that I should even ask.

"Upset?" he said. "I just got to spend three hours in a pitch-dark elevator." As if that explained it.

When I pressed him further, he continued, "There was nowhere to go. Nothing to look at or listen to. No distractions. It was perfect. How often do you get a chance like that to work on your prayer?"

I remember thinking to myself at the time that there was some sort of real power at work in that monk—a capacity for joy even under the most trying conditions—and that if I could learn to live like him, I could be a happy man.

When one learns to be content with the lowliest and worst of everything—not just resigned, but content—then there is never a wasted moment. There is no such thing as a dull, futile, or useless experience. Every sorrow loses its sting, because everything is an opportunity to glorify God. Saint Paul wrote, "For the sake of Christ, then, I am content with weaknesses, insults, hardships, persecutions, and calamities; for when I am weak, then I am strong" (2 Cor 12:10). Once you have learned to find contentment in adversity, all of life becomes charged with light and hope and joy.

HOMEWORK: Laugh with someone who laughs at you.

~

SERENITY IN WORD

No community is without friction. Therefore the morning and evening prayers should never end without the Our Father. The superior himself should say it in front of everyone so that the brethren will be reminded of their promise when they say "Forgive us as we forgive others."

—Chapter 13: Weekday Prayers

You can't be serene and resentful at the same time. The two are absolutely incompatible. If a true Christian is insulted or scorned, he says to himself, "Well, I'm sure I had it coming. Now how can I help fix this?"

Not long ago, I was working in the library when two of the novices walked in laughing and talking. I snapped at them. Immediately, they both went silent. Then one of them whispered, "I'm so sorry, Brother. You must have had a hard day." What serenity he had! Instead of focusing on his own hurt feelings, he immediately turned his attention to me and my suffering.

But not all of us are quite so disposed to serenity as that novice, so Saint Benedict insists on saying the Our Father at the beginning and at the end of the day, because when you've got this many guys

living together, there's bound to be some disagreements—even very serious ones. We need, therefore, to remind ourselves to forgive one another before the day even starts. Then we need to do it again at the end of the day to be sure we've lived up to that promise. This is an easy monkish practice for anyone to adopt, and I highly recommend it. At the end of the day, take an inventory of all the people who have angered you, and forgive them. Say it out loud. Then you can go to bed.

Mind you, forgiveness doesn't mean hiding your anger or covering it up with pleasant feelings. Forgiveness is an act of the will, so whether you feel like it or not, you have in fact forgiven your enemies the moment you ask God for the strength to do so. The feelings will follow later, and so will the serenity.

HOMEWORK: Deliberately walk (or drive) behind someone slow.

∼

SERENITY IN DEED

A monk should not chase after pleasures.

—Chapter 4: The Tools of Good Works

o what's wrong with pleasures? Why not chase after them? Does Benedict want his monks to be miserable?

It may sound like that at first, but the longer you live by Saint Benedict's advice, the more sense it makes. When you take pleasure in something (food, music, art, sport, film . . .), the experience is agreeable but temporary. There's nothing wrong with seeking out such experiences. In fact, the Bible recommends it: "I commend enjoyment, for man has no good thing under the sun but to eat and drink and enjoy himself." (Eccl 8:15). So clearly there's nothing wrong with having fun. But take note of that crucial stipulation, "under the sun". Presumably, there are things even more worthy of seeking beyond the sun—like Heaven, virtue, truth, and above all, God. When we start to *chase* after pleasures, we confuse our priorities and become "lovers of pleasure rather than lovers of God" (2 Tim 3:4).

Think for a moment of the rich young man whom Jesus tried to recruit in the Gospel of Mark.

He went away sad, Mark tells us, because he had many possessions (10:22). The guy in that story refused a direct request from Jesus Himself simply because he was too preoccupied with his stuff.

The students at my school often ask me why I quit being a beach lifeguard. Wasn't that more fun than being a monk? Well, yes, in some respects. But in defense of my decision, I can say this: There's nothing more depressing than a forty-year-old lifeguard. Everyone comes to a point in his life when he must choose between fun and joy. And to choose the former over the latter leads to a whole lot of emptiness. These decisions aren't always life-changing, but they do have a cumulative effect; and they are often very difficult because joy takes work. Ironically, the rich young man went away sad because he threw in his lot with fun. When it comes to the bigger life decisions, we must have the wisdom to choose joy, no matter how fun the alternative.

HOMEWORK: Give up thirty minutes of television or video games, and read the Bible instead.

~

SELF-ABASEMENT

Believe in your heart that you are an unworthy servant of God, humbling yourself and saying with the Prophet: "I am a worm, and no man; scorned by men, and despised by the people" (Ps 22:6).

Every human being is infinitely loved and infinitely precious. We haven't earned that divine dignity; it is a gift. Nonetheless, we convince ourselves that we must somehow show ourselves worthy of God's love—that if we are charming or charitable or brave enough, He will feel obliged to reward us. Self-abasement is the antidote to this delusion. It is the practice of reminding ourselves that we are nothing without God's grace and will never earn it. Ironically, this healthy sense of nothingness, understood correctly, brings with it a deeper sense of confidence and freedom. As Janice Joplin said, "Freedom's just another word for nothing left to lose."

SELF-ABASEMENT IN THOUGHT

As soon as evil thoughts come into your heart, dash them against Christ.

—Chapter 4: The Tools of Good Works

ot to be confused with self-loathing or self-hatred (for who would dare hate any of God's creations), genuine self-abasement represents an advanced stage of spiritual development. In a chapter entitled "Self-Abasement in the Sight of God", Thomas à Kempis summed it up this way: "Left to myself, I am nothing but total weakness. But if You look upon me for an instant, I am at once made strong and filled with new joy."[1] Thomas à Kempis can feel secure precisely because the burden of resisting sin does not rest on him alone. He knows that when temptation comes, he has only to dash that sin against the Rock who is Jesus Christ.[2]

---

[1] Thomas à Kempis, *The Imitation of Christ*, The Work of God Apostolate, theworkofgod.org/Library/Books/Kempis/Imitation_Jesus_Christ.htm.

[2] This image actually comes from one of the more disturbing verses of the cursing psalms: "Happy shall he be who takes your little ones and dashes them against the rock!" (137:9). Literally, the psalmist is asking God to kill his enemy's children. Well, we all feel like that from time to time—or most of us do anyway—

and it's good that there's a prayer for people who feel that way. But Saint Benedict sees the "children" as temptations and "Babylon" as Satan's kingdom. He envisions us dashing these temptations against Christ Himself, who stands just to our left on the spiritual battlefield, unflinching and rock-solid.

At times, you may become discouraged when you pray because your sins seem to jump out at you. You may actually feel worse than ever. But don't let that get you down. It's actually a sign of progress because the closer you draw to the perfect holiness of God, the more your own imperfections will stand out against the pure light of His holiness. It's like standing next to a sky-scraper: The closer you stand, the smaller you feel. This explains why really holy people are often the last ones to admit it, because the holier they get, the less holy they feel (so I've heard).

True self-esteem, therefore, is always accompanied by self-abasement because knowing your limits is so crucial to knowing yourself. Goethe—who, I should add, would be distressed to hear his words used in this context by a Catholic monk—wrote: "The discerning man who acknowledges his limitations is not far off perfection."[3] The truth is that we are all sick with sin and Jesus is the only cure.

HOMEWORK: Thank God for something you are not good at.

～

---

[3] Johann Wolfgang von Goethe, *Maxims and Reflections* (New York: MacMillan, 1906), 518, Project Gutenberg, gutenberg.org/files/33670/33670-h/33670-h.htm.

SELF-ABASEMENT IN WORD

Do not desire to be called holy before you are;
but be holy first, that you may be truly so called.

—Chapter 4: The Tools of Good Works

aint Benedict, it appears, was comfortable with the idea that his monks might want to be *called* holy. But what place can ambition have in a monastery of all places, where one comes to pursue a life of humility and self-denial? Isn't this vainglory? Saint Benedict doesn't seem to think so. And he has the Scriptures to back him up. In his letter to Timothy, Saint Paul himself boasts: "I have fought the good fight, I have finished the race, I have kept the faith. From now on, there is laid up for me the crown of righteousness" (2 Tim 4:7).

At first glance, language like this can be confusing, because we tend to equate humility with self-deprecation: "Oh, it was nothing, really", "Oh, it's just something I threw together", or my own personal favorite: "I'm the biggest sinner of them all", which actually turns out to be a form of boasting, doesn't it? Self-abasement is not self-deprecation, but self-knowledge. So if you really are good at something, it is no act of humility to belittle your talents. When you do that, you just wind up

insulting God, who gave you those talents in the first place.

At Oxford, I had a friend who lived in a castle, who invited me to stay with his family for a few days during one of our breaks. As we pulled up his driveway, and I saw this enormous piece of architecture that he calls "home"—complete with its own pond, tennis courts, golf course, and chapel —I looked over at his mom and said, "Seriously? That's your *home*?" His mom looked at the castle and then at me and then back at the castle again and said, "Yes, it's wonderful, isn't it? We really are blessed." I might have expected her to say something like "Well, it needs work" or "Thanks, but it's really hard to keep up." Instead, she looked at her castle and thanked God for it. That is true humility.

So when folks praise God for some gift that you have, there is no sin in acknowledging the gift. In fact, it would be a sin to deny it. "It is a sign of humility if a man does not think too much of himself," wrote Thomas Aquinas, "but if a man condemns the good things he has received from God, this, far from being a proof of humility, shows him to be ungrateful."[4]

HOMEWORK: Thank God for something you're good at.

～

[4] Thomas Aquinas, *Summa Theologica*, trans. Fathers of the English Dominican Province, II-II, q. 35, a. 1. www.documentacathol icaomnia.eu/03d/1225-1274,_Thomas_Aquinas,_Summa_Theolo giae_%5B1%5D,_EN.pdf.

SELF-ABASEMENT IN DEED

No one should be excused from kitchen duty, because this is how merit and charity are acquired. Also, the servers should wash the linens at the end of the week and do the Saturday cleaning. Both the outgoing and the incoming servers should wash the feet of all.

—Chapter 35: Kitchen Duty

veryone has chores to do, and nobody—not even a monk—likes to do them. Even so, someone's got to clean the house, make the beds, take out the trash, do the dishes, mow the lawn . . . If these jobs aren't done, your home quickly becomes a dirty, stinky, ugly mess. Thus, dish duty may sound like a minor detail, but it is essential to the good order of the community. And precisely because dishwashing is the job nobody wants, Benedict sees it as a unique opportunity to acquire "merit and charity." By having the servers wash the feet of the brethren, he links their work with that of Christ Himself, who "came not to be served but to serve" (Mt 20:28).

We don't have to work wonders, cast out demons, raise the dead, levitate, bilocate, have visions, or make prophesies to be a saint. Thérèse of Lisieux

wrote that the Lord "needs neither our brilliant deeds nor our beautiful thoughts." Rather, "He loves simplicity."[5] Or, in the words of Mother Teresa: "There are no great deeds. Only small deeds with great love."

So what may seem like a small act of service is really a big opportunity to cultivate holiness—an opportunity of which no monk should be deprived.

[5] Thérèse of Lisieux, *The Story of a Soul*, www.gutenberg.org/ebooks/16772.

"Whatever you do," wrote Saint Paul, "do all to the glory of God" (1 Cor 10:31). That means you can wash dishes for the glory of God, take a walk for the glory of God, brush your teeth for the glory of God, play soccer or change a light bulb for the glory of God. Whatever you do, you can do it for the glory of God.

It's not easy, but if you want to cultivate a genuine sense of self-esteem, you must learn to recognize these little acts of self-abasement for what they are: big opportunities to cultivate humility.

HOMEWORK: Clean a toilet.

∼

PRUDENCE

*Only do what is lawful, and follow the example
of your elders.*

Before you start breaking the rules, be sure you
know why those rules exist in the first place. A
good rule, like a good fence, is there to protect you.
In the words of Saint Paul, your thoughts should
be wholly directed to whatever is true, honorable,
just, pure, lovely, gracious, excellent, and worthy
of praise (Phil 4:8). A prudent person knows when
to keep an open mind and when to close it.

PRUDENCE IN THOUGHT

The monk should fulfill daily the commands of God by works; he should love chastity, and he should hate no one.

— Chapter 4: The Tools of Good Works

The first time I read Benedict's advice on chastity, it struck me as extremely odd. Perhaps this is because I associate the term "chastity" with all the things I shouldn't do. And from what I can tell, that's how most people think of it. When I teach moral theology, my students inevitably ask, "When I'm on a date, how far can I go before it's a sin?" But a question like this demonstrates a certain lack of prudence. After all, you would never ask a teacher, "What's the least amount of work I can do to pass this class?" And you would certainly never ask your coach, "What's the slowest I can run this race?" So if your goal is to get to Heaven, then asking, "What's the least I can do?", probably indicates that you have the wrong attitude. A better way to put it might be, "What is the best way to be chaste on a date?" Or better still, "How can a young man keep his way pure?" (Ps 119:9)

Of course, there are many different ways of answering this question. When our Brother Athanasius teaches the unit on chastity, he walks into the classroom and writes ''NO'' on the chalkboard. Then he says, ''Today we're going to talk about chastity. Any questions?''

Sooner or later, someone raises his hand and says, "Is it ok if we . . ."

"No."

"But what if she's . . ."

"No."

"Sometimes if I . . ."

"No."

"But what if we're . . ."

"No. If you have to ask the question, the answer is no."

His point, I think, is that when you are attracted to someone, there is a certain line that separates a chaste exchange of affection from the pursuit of lust. Naturally, we all want to get as close to that line as we can without crossing it; and when we start asking questions like these, it's because we want to push that line a little further and are looking for a good excuse.

But Saint Benedict says to *love* chastity. How do you love something that is always "no"? Anything good is loveable, after all, and chastity is good. So here's how I put it: Feel free to do anything you could brag about to your mom. Would your mother approve? If so, then you are probably good to go.

HOMEWORK: Think of a rule you don't like, and re-word it in a positive way.

~

PRUDENCE IN WORD

If any monk, without the permission of the abbot, presumes to associate with an excommunicated brother in any way, let him be excommunicated as well.

—Chapter 26: Those Who Associate with the Excommunicated

They say the road to Hell is paved with good intentions. If you ask me, I think it's more likely to be paved with bad intentions, but the fact remains that people sometimes do very bad things for the very best reasons. When I was working on the Beach Patrol, I was told a story about a boy who slipped off the Fifty-Third Street Pier and drowned. Instead of signaling the lifeguard (who was no more than twenty yards away), his father jumped in after him, and pulled him to shore by the hair. As it turned out, the child had broken his neck in the fall. He might well have survived, but his spinal cord was severed when his father tugged on his hair. Tragic. Avoidable. And a classic example of what theologians call "a misdirected good".

Even compassion can do harm when you show it in the wrong way. And the only guarantee against making that kind of mistake is the virtue of obe-

dience. Granted, there are times when we are called upon to resist authority. But most of the time, we have to trust that these authorities—secular authorities like our teachers and parents, government authorities like police and firefighters, or religious authorities like abbots and pastors—know what they're doing and know more than we do.[1] I realize that's hard to hear, but Saint Paul himself says, "Let every person be subject to the governing authorities. For there is no authority except from God, and those that exist have been instituted by God" (Rom 13:1).

In the situation described by Saint Benedict, the

---

[1] I find it baffling how people are so quick to accept the voice of authority when it comes to medicine, law, plumbing, dentistry, and auto repair, but consider themselves experts when it comes to theology.

offending monk certainly *thinks* he is doing the right thing by consoling the excommunicated. But he doesn't have the whole picture, does he? Only the abbot knows for certain why he was excommunicated and how he is suffering. Encouragement may be the last thing he needs. Saint John Cassian warns that a monk who associates with the excommunicated "only encourages more arrogance and stubbornness in the offender. By giving him a consolation that is only hurtful, he makes his heart still harder."[2] In other words, you don't help a sick person when you encourage his sickness. So in a situation like this, the prudent response is to pray. Come to think of it, prayer is always the most prudent response to anything.

HOMEWORK: Just say "thank you" the next time someone tells you something you already know.

~

---

[2] John Cassian, *The Twelve Books on the Institutes of the Coenobi* 2, 16, translated by author.

PRUDENCE IN DEED

Choose a prudent man to be cellarer of the mon-astery—someone of settled habits, temperate and frugal. Above all, he should be humble, so that whenever he receives a request, he will answer with a kind word, for it is written: "Does not a word surpass a good gift?" (Sir 18:17).

—Chapter 31: The Cellarer

It is the job of the cellarer to keep track of all the monastery's material goods. This is a very powerful office, which is why it is so important that the abbot choose for the job a monk who is humble, frugal, and prudent. Material things can be a great temptation, even in a spiritual community (see the story of Judas in the Gospels), so the cellarer has to be the sort of person who can watch over worldly goods without becoming worldly himself.

What's more, the things themselves have a certain sacredness of their own. Throughout the centuries, Christians have slipped into the error of believing that our existence could be neatly divided between the spiritual and the physical—that the spiritual world was good and the physical world

was bad. To be sure, the spiritual is more important than the physical (see Col 3:2); but you can't just dismiss the physical world altogether because, as soon as you do that, you become capable of abusing it. And if God said that His creation was good (Gen 1:31), who are we to say otherwise?

When I was seventeen, I burned a hole in the living room carpet. I didn't do it on purpose, but let's just say I wasn't thinking when I set the hot kettle of popcorn on the rug in front of the TV. A few minutes later, my mother was standing before me with tears in her eyes, saying, "How much of this house do you plan to destroy before you finally leave for college? Just let me know so I won't get too attached." That was a few weeks after I had decided to juggle bowling balls in my bedroom, and several months after I had backed the family car into the garage door. I didn't intend to do any of those things, but then again, it's easy to be sloppy with someone else's stuff. Saint Benedict foresees this danger in his monastery, where no one owns anything. So he devotes three full chapters to the care of material goods.

Ultimately, everything we have is on loan to us from God. Before long, we'll be dead and someone else will be in charge of it. And this holds true on a global scale as well because "the earth is the LORD's" (Ps 24:1). So regardless of how you feel about climate change or species extinction or resource depletion, the material world should be treated with enormous care because it doesn't belong to us. We have no more right to burn a hole in the ozone layer than to burn a hole in the living room carpet. It's a matter of respect—not for nature itself, but for God, nature's Architect and Lord.

HOMEWORK: Clean up someone else's mess. Bonus points if it's on the floor.

~

SILENCE

Only speak when you are spoken to, for Scripture says, "When words are many, transgression is not lacking" (Prov 10:19).

It can be a great temptation to fill every silence with words—even when we are praying. But for Saint Benedict, there is no such thing as an awkward silence. Instead, he sees every moment of quiet as an opportunity to listen to God.

124

SILENCE IN THOUGHT

*Listen, my son, to the teachings of the master,
and incline the ear of your heart.*
— Prologue

*L*isten. The first word of the *Rule* of Saint Benedict is also the most important. For the monk, it represents the focus of the spiritual life: listening to God. Everything a monk does—from the way he eats and sleeps to the way he works and prays—is designed to help him listen.

"Are you listening to me?"

"Can't you hear what I'm trying to say?"

People use these expressions all the time when they are arguing. Just think how many problems would be solved if we really did listen to one another. A Benedictine nun by the name of Sister Makrina once told me that I should never answer a complaint without repeating it back to the person who made it. Why? Because it assures the speaker that you are listening. You can't force people to listen to you, but you would be surprised how open they become once they are convinced that you are listening to them.

The monk's life, however, is not so much about listening to other people as it is about listening to

God. And that's even more difficult because God is a gentleman. He speaks very, very quietly and rarely forces anyone to listen to Him. If we are not vigilant, we can easily mistake some other voice—or even our own voice—for His. This is why it's so important to share your spiritual journey with someone old and wise—a mentor who can help you distinguish the true voice of God from the many imposters who want to take His place.

I'll leave you with something else Sister Makrina told me: When you meet a wise person, listen to him and you will learn wisdom; when you meet a foolish person, listen to him and you will learn patience; when you are alone, listen to God, and you will learn everything else.

HOMEWORK: Refrain from having the last word in your next conversation (even if it's friendly).

~

SILENCE IN WORD

Let us do what the Prophet says: "I will guard my ways, that I may not sin with my tongue" (Ps 39:1). Because silence is so precious, the monk should rarely speak even for good and holy reasons.

— Chapter 6: Silence

ather Timothy Horner is the oldest monk at my monastery. He's six foot two, with a patch of red hair sprouting from his head like a moss. He's been all around the world, has two degrees in classics from Oxford, served with the British Special Forces in India during World War II, and is one of the founders of Saint Louis Abbey. He is the direct descendent of "Little" Jack Horner (remember the nursery rhyme?), and he is the most noble man I have ever met. I've never heard Father Timothy raise his voice, I've never heard him use more words than were necessary, and I've never seen him visibly upset by anything.

During my novitiate, I took a class from him on Saint Benedict's *Rule* (which he has translated). Father Timothy was always early for these classes, and I was often late—huffing and puffing, pages of notebook paper flying, a ready excuse on the tip of my tongue. But on one occasion, Father Timothy

was late for class. I made sure all my notes and books were in order, and was rehearsing a rebuke for him when he arrived. He never gave me the chance to use it. He made no excuses or apologies. In fact, he didn't say anything at all as he strode into the room. Instead, he laid his books on the table and placed a small yellow square of paper in my hand. On it, these words were written: "God's first language is silence: all else is translation."[1]

Isn't it a shame that we live in a society that so

[1] Thomas Keating, *Invitation to Love: The Way of Christian Contemplation*.

fears silence. We turn the radios on in our rooms, the TVs on in our dens, the stereos on in our cars, and when we are not near any of these places, we plug iPods into our ears—anything to avoid silence. Yet silence itself is the language of God! I'll let you in on something I just recently learned: set aside a few minutes each day to just be silent, and you will find that you instantly become a more peaceful person. Imagine Jesus saying to you (as He said to His disciples), "Come with me by yourself to a quiet place" (cf. Mk 6:31).

HOMEWORK: Drive somewhere with the radio and the cell phone turned off.

~

SILENCE IN DEED

While the monks are eating, someone should read aloud from a book. In church at the start of the week, the reader should ask everyone to pray for him that God may ward off the spirit of pride.

— Chapter 38: The Weekly Readers

ilence is so important to monks that they don't even talk while they are eating. Instead, one of them reads from a book while the others quietly have their meal. Saint Benedict even stipulates that the brethren should use sign language rather than whisper when they need something. In my monastery, we have special signs for milk, water, bread, butter, starch, salt, pepper, and so on. The sign for water is three fingers. The sign for starch is a closed fist. We even have a sign for ketchup, which we make by dragging the right forefinger across the left wrist. It's weird, but it works. And it shows that we really mean it when we say that silence is precious.

Because the reader is the center of attention at meals, he needs to be particularly on guard against the sin of pride. This is a temptation common to ministers of all kinds because when you are good at something, it's easy to take credit for it. Worse

still, you can wind up putting your personality at the center of your ministry. Have you ever listened to a preacher who sounded like he was hosting a talk show? "Well hello, everyone! Good morning! The Lord be with you!" Every sentence must end with an exclamation point!

When the minister keeps inserting himself between God and us, we get angry. So a good minister (like a good musician or a good writer or a good teacher) knows in his heart that the ministry comes first—the message, the music, the story comes first

—and the minister's personality takes a far-distant second. Granted, this is hard to do because we can speak only from our own experience. But if we pray humbly, the Holy Spirit should make up for that weakness (Rom 8:26).

Mother Teresa used to refer to herself as "God's pencil stub". She didn't deny that she was accomplishing great works, but she gave credit for those works to the Holy Spirit, who held the pencil. "Will the axe boast over the one who swings it?" asked the prophet Isaiah (10:15). You may be sharp, but give credit where credit is due. And if you want your creation to last, don't build it around yourself. Build it around Christ (1 Cor 3:11).

HOMEWORK: The next time someone compliments you, give God the credit.

~

DIGNITY

Do not be too quick to laugh, for it is written: "A fool raises his voice when he laughs" (Sir 21:20).

When you can control your laughter, you are beginning to develop true human dignity. This goes far beyond mere self-denial, because it means you have to know not only how to restrain yourself, but when and how to indulge yourself as well.

DIGNITY IN THOUGHT

We believe that God is present everywhere and that the eyes of the Lord see the good and the bad in every place (Prov 15:3). Therefore, we should always keep in mind how we ought to behave in the sight of God and His angels, and let us so stand to sing, that our minds may be in harmony with our voices.

—Chapter 19: The Practice
of the Presence of God

When the White Queen of Wonderland tells Alice that she is one hundred years old, Alice replies, "I *can't* believe *that* . . . one *can't* believe impossible things."

"I daresay you haven't had much practice" is the White Queen's reply. "When I was your age, I always did it for half an hour a day. Why, sometimes I've believed as many as six impossible things before breakfast."

The deepest mysteries of the Christian Faith (the Incarnation, the Trinity, the Creation, the angels . . .) are incomprehensible but not illogical—and certainly not impossible. Nonetheless, contemplating these mysteries can give your brain a workout. Many Christians just quit trying and lose their faith altogether.

When I was in graduate school, I took a class on Renaissance literature. I remember that one of the students in the class asked the professor a question about *Paradise Lost*.

"Did the author consider this fantasy?" he asked.

"No," said the professor. "The thing you have to remember about people back then is that they were extremely superstitious. They really believed there were angels and demons all around them, fighting for their souls."

The young man laughed and said, "Imagine that!"

Then a female student behind me raised her hand and said, "I don't have to imagine that. I believe it."

Certainly Saint Benedict believed it as well, but it is a belief that is easy to forget. Seeing, as they say, is believing; and these days, folks tend to think that if something can't be measured or touched, then it must not exist.[1] Well, we may not see God, but He surely sees us, and He sees everything we do—even the stuff we are ashamed of. All around us, His angels are protecting our souls (Ps 91:11). And this isn't just my old-fashioned opinion. This is a belief that is as old as the Bible itself. There are demons and angels all around us. We really believe this.

But do we act like it? To be sure, God has a sense of humor. Otherwise, what would be the point of the turkey buzzard? Or the armadillo? Or the naked mole rat? But are there some things we wouldn't laugh at if we knew He and His angels were watching? Bearing this in mind is the best way to preserve your dignity as a child of God.

HOMEWORK: Spend half an hour reading Thomas Aquinas' philosophical treatise on angels. It will blow your mind.

～

---

[1] Unless of course, they are talking about quantum physics, relativity, dark energy, electrons, and such, in which case, they suddenly and inexplicably believe it.

DIGNITY IN WORD

Guard your tongue against vulgar or wicked words, do not love excessive talking, watch how you joke around, and avoid unrestrained or raucous laughter.

—Chapter 4: The Tools of Good Works

I almost never regret keeping my mouth shut, but I frequently regret opening it. And when the time comes for an apology, it's sad how often I hear myself saying, "Gosh, I was only joking." Saint Benedict wants his monks to be very careful with their sense of humor. Laughter can be life-affirming, but it can also break people down, filling their heads with vulgar or cruel images.

Take my college roommates, for example. For two years, I lived in a house with seven other rugby players. We teased one another incessantly, and that was okay because, frankly, it was part of the fun of living with seven rugby players. If any one of us said, did, or implied anything even slightly embarrassing, he could expect to become the butt of every joke in the house. Those were the rules, and we all understood them. It was practically in the lease.

One of the guys (his last name was Ackerman,

so we called him "Ack") had a habit of posting little signs everywhere. It was funny because he was six foot six inches and 280 pounds, but he was also kind of a neat freak. The signs said things like "Please wash your coffee mugs" and "Don't forget to take the lint out of the dryer." As you can imagine, no one obeyed the signs. In fact, I don't think we even noticed them at first; but pretty soon, we started to put up little signs of our own saying things like "Remember to recycle your earwax" and "Please do not eat the socks." Then we started leaving little notes for one another with messages like, "Rudy, I cooked your cat. Leftovers in the fridge" and "Will, your sister called. She wants her Barbies back." Someone left a note by the phone that just said, "Ack". Then someone else wrote underneath it, "your mom" and later, someone else came along and wrote "is dead". What none of us knew was that Ack's mother had gone to the emergency room earlier that week with chest pains, so when Ack came home and saw the message, he panicked. He was halfway to the hospital before he realized it was a joke. That was the end of the funny signs. And it might have been the end of all six roommates if Ack hadn't been such a nice guy.

There is a line that can be crossed when you tell a joke, and it is often difficult to know exactly where that line is. The funniest jokes, after all, are those that come right up to the line of impropriety without actually crossing it. This is why—and here's the serious part—you really need to make sure you know who you are teasing and how the person will take it. You can't really know for sure what is in another man's heart; so just because your friend is laughing along, that doesn't necessarily mean he's feeling all right. What's more, some jokes are simply beneath your dignity.[2]

HOMEWORK: Make someone smile without making them laugh.

∼

[2] For the record, jokes about race, religious convictions, and family should be avoided entirely.

DIGNITY IN DEED

We are reluctant to dictate the quantity of food for others. However, allowing for the weakness of the sick, we think one hemina of wine per day should be sufficient for each because "wine makes even wise men act like fools" (Sir 19:2).

—Chapter 40: Food and Drink

Just as undignified humor and excessive laughter are symptoms of spiritual illness, so is immoderate drinking. Saint Benedict preferred that his monks abstain from alcohol entirely. But if the monks wouldn't give up drinking altogether, he insisted they should at least drink responsibly—no more than a single *hemina* per day.

As you can imagine, the exact measure of the *hemina* is a topic hotly debated by monks all around the world. It could be anything from a cup to three quarters of a gallon. But one thing is certain: wine meant something entirely different to monks of the Middle Ages than it does today. For starters, alcohol wasn't entirely recreational. Wine made dirty water drinkable, so unless you had a very clean well, your survival depended on it. Even children drank wine. Nonetheless, I find it amusing that Benedict

143

tried—and failed—to talk his monks out of recreational drinking.

Similarly, I operate under no illusions when it comes to teenage alcohol consumption. It's a problem, to be sure. But drinking isn't the only teen appetite that can get out of hand. Video games, texting, and television—even dieting and exercise can evolve into something destructive.

I have a friend who claims he once spent thirty-six straight hours playing *World of Warcraft*, breaking only for bathroom and pizza runs. Honestly, this can't be healthy. Our dignity exceeds that of the animals precisely because we have the capacity to control our appetites. We set limits for ourselves, and if we can't meet those limitations by virtue of our own self-control, we enlist the help of friends and family. One of my students invented an ingenious solution to his late-night gaming: every evening at seven, he would hand the computer cord to his dad. When his laptop battery ran out, he knew he had reached his limit. It wasn't very good for his laptop, but it was good for his soul.

HOMEWORK: Spend an entire day without looking at a screen.

~

DON'T
BE
THE
LIFE
OF
THE
PARTY

BE YOURSELF

DISCRETION

If you must speak, do so gently, humbly, earnestly, and quietly, with few and sensible words; for it is written: "The wise man is known by the fewness of his words."

As the saying goes, it's better to remain silent and be thought a fool, than to open your mouth and remove all doubt. But there are occasions when you simply must speak up. At times like these, you need to have a well-formed sense of discretion.

DISCRETION IN THOUGHT

No monk should defend another in the mona-
stery. Nor should he take sides in an argument
because it causes very grave scandal. If anyone
should violate this rule, let him be severely pun-
ished.

—Chapter 69: Presuming
to Defend a Brother

ow. Severely punished. And just for defending a friend. There's got to be more here than meets the eye. And of course, there is. Saint Benedict is talking about cliques and the grumbling that inevitably accompanies them. When you take sides in an argument (not a discussion, mind you, but a genuine quarrel), you turn a personal problem into a public one. A disagreement that might well have been settled in private must now be resolved in public.

But what makes this behavior even more deplorable is that you are, on a personal level, playing God. Jesus said, "Judge not, that you be not judged" (Mt 7:1). By this, of course, He did not mean that we should just accept everyone's behavior. We are called to make judgments about particular acts. We are permitted—obliged, in fact—to analyze certain moral acts and determine whether

they conform to objective moral standards. We are obliged to say, "This or that act is sinful" even "This or that person committed a sinful act." What we are forbidden to say is, "This is a bad person" or "This person is going to Hell." The distinction is subtle, but necessary. We judge acts, not people. This is why taking sides in a fight is so dangerous. As the saying goes, "He who meddles in a quarrel not his own is like one who takes a passing dog by the ears" (Prov 26:17). How do you decide which brothers are worth defending? Just the ones you agree with? The smartest ones? The ones you like the most? And are you sure you know all the details? Once you start judging your friends, there's no telling where your judging will end.

Here's the catch, though: You don't judge people when they're in the wrong, but you don't judge them when they're in the right either. In the old days, people seemed pretty confident their neighbors were going to Hell. These days, people seem pretty confident they're going to Heaven. Either way, it's not our call. Above all, discretion means knowing when to keep your opinion to yourself.

HOMEWORK: The next time someone annoys you, don't tell anyone.

～

DISCRETION IN WORD

Let the cellarer of the monastery be in charge of all the monastery goods. If a brother makes a stupid request, the cellarer shouldn't sadden him with a cold refusal, but politely and humbly tell him no.

—Chapter 31: The Cellarer

I love this bit of the *Rule* because my students ask me stupid questions all the time. At nine o'clock the night before a paper is due I get an email asking if I can recommend sources; I get a letter from a parent demanding the rationale behind a grade I assigned two months ago. Another student asks for a 7 A.M. help session when he doesn't even do his homework. But what really gets my goat is when a student asks for something he doesn't need *as though he deserved it*. I once had a seventh-grader tell me, "This isn't what we pay you for." (As though *he* ever paid *me* for anything.)

Of course, this is not a problem unique to teachers. Policemen, referees, checkout clerks, and secretaries deal with it all the time. As a lifeguard in Galveston, I used to marvel at the stupidity of the average beachgoer: parents napped while their children swam in the rip current, tourists tried to eat dead fish they found on the sand, swimmers ran

screaming from the surf when they spotted a dolphin. While pointing at the horizon, a guy once asked me if "that thing" was Mexico. He couldn't figure out why the water "just stopped".

To be sure, it is a great temptation to answer with sarcasm or anger when someone makes an unreasonable demand. But what good would that do? And whom would it help? Besides, aren't we always making unreasonable demands of God? We sleep through class, skip the homework, and pray for an A on the test. Yet we are infuriated when we get a bad grade. Or we ask for a miracle, then chalk it up to coincidence when we get it.

God responds to our stupidity with kindness, patience, love, and generosity. Imagine if He answered, ''Three hundred people just died in a factory fire in Cambodia. You think I really care what grade you make on your history test? Come back when you have a *real* problem.'' Instead, He says, ''Don't worry. Every hair on your head has been counted'' (Mt 10:31). God is infinite, so you can be sure that some small part of Him really cares whether you pass your history test. And that part is infinite too.

HOMEWORK: Find a point of agreement with someone who has a different opinion.

∼

DISCRETION IN DEED

The extent of an excommunication should be determined by the seriousness of the offense as well as the prudence of the abbot. And it should continue until the disobedient monk has made satisfaction.

—Chapter 24: Different
Kinds of Excommunication

ere's a joke: A guy with a wooden eye goes to a disco and sees a beautiful woman standing at the bar. She happens to have a peg leg. He walks up and asks her to dance. She says, "Would I!"

He says, "I didn't want to dance with you anyway, peg leg!"[1]

There's a moral to this joke: Anger has its uses, but before you act in anger, make sure you understand why other people act the way they do. Saint Benedict says that a monk shouldn't be quick to laugh. But he shouldn't be quick to lash out either. More important still, he should understand his own motives. Saint Benedict clearly believes that fairness and proportion are intrinsic to the good order of a community. I would add that they are also intrinsic to the good order of an individual.

---

[1] Say the joke out loud if you don't get it.

155

When we are angry or depressed, we need to be able to take a step back and ask ourselves whether our mood actually matches the reality around us. To put it in more psychological terms, we need to verify that the response matches the stimulus. If someone cuts you off on the highway and you are bent out of shape for the rest of the day; if your brother breaks your hockey stick, and you can't stop thinking how much you want to get even; if a friend doesn't invite you to a party, and you spend the rest of the weekend wondering what's wrong —don't just explain it away with, "He's a jerk." You won't learn anything from that. Instead, try to sort through why *your* reaction is so extreme.

Our friend with the wooden eye clearly has some

deep insecurities, but everyone has something that triggers a negative response. When you figure out why this or that behavior bothers you, then you will be able to set about restoring peace and balance in your own life. Here again I recommend finding a mentor who can act as a sort of referee between you and your moods and can help you figure out why you feel the way you do, and how to come to terms with it.

Like the disobedient monk, when you get upset, you may need to "excommunicate" yourself for a while—go off by yourself and cool down. Afterward you might need to make up in some practical way for the damage you've done. Whatever the case, remember that the goal is to restore harmony. An excessive penance—even if you give it to yourself—will just throw the balance off in a different direction. Pray for the gift of discernment.

HOMEWORK: Let yourself be interrupted in a conversation, and don't finish what you were going to say unless someone asks.

∼

REVERENCE

Wherever you go, bow your head in prayer, remembering the words of the publican: "God, be merciful to me a sinner!" (Lk 18:13).

Here in the final step, Saint Benedict describes an ancient monastic practice known as *custodia oculorum*—custody of the eyes. These days, we would call it simply "reverence", and we save this virtue for last because it is the sum of all the others. The fear of God that we strive for in the first step inspires self-denial and obedience. Perseverance in those practices, tempered by sincere repentance for our failures, strengthens us to experience serenity in the face of adversity. This in turn finds expression in self-abasement, prudence, and, finally, silence. Now silence, infused with dignity and discretion, culminates in a profound and joyful reverence for creation, for our neighbor, for ourselves, and for God. Life becomes a constant prayer whereby we discover our fullest dignity as brothers and sisters of Christ.

REVERENCE IN THOUGHT

*Even when a monk is away from his monastery,
he should perform the Work of God in holy fear
and on bended knee wherever he happens to be.*

—Chapter 50: A Monk on a Trip

There are two types of men who join a monastery: those for whom the *Rule* suits their character, and those for whom it tames their character. The first sort have no need of a command to say their prayers. They will naturally say their prayers when the time comes, whether or not they are in the presence of the community. For the rest of us, though, it takes real vigilance to keep those hours from slipping by. And it's especially hard to keep it up when no one is watching. Sometimes the prayers feel like a chore, and we can't wait to get them over with so we can go back to whatever we were doing. This is why we join a monastery and wear funny-looking clothes. The rules and reminders and rituals are necessary because, without them, we are likely to backslide.

Saint Benedict was all too familiar with the second type of man, and so he adds this reminder that, even when monks are on their own, they need to say their prayers with the same devotion as they

would have in the monastery—not just muttering them to themselves while doing something else, but fulfilling the obligation "in holy fear and on bended knee".

When you are away from home, your parents expect you to call them every now and then to let them know what you are doing. That way they won't worry too much, and you won't fall out of touch. And so it is with your Heavenly Father. Prayer is a way of "calling home". It keeps you in touch with your Father and in touch with your spiritual community. "Draw near to God," writes Saint James, "and he will draw near to you" (Jas 4:8).

When I first arrived at Saint Louis Abbey as a postulant, there was an old, senile monk named Edward, who carried a little silver bell with him wherever he went. It wasn't long before my curiosity got the better of me and I asked him why.

"At my age, the mind becomes increasingly undependable," he answered, "so I carry this bell with me. Whenever I get lost, I just ring it. Then I know exactly where I am."

Let the name of Jesus be that silver bell for you —a reminder of who you are, where you stand, and what you stand for. Then, in the midst of all the chaos of life, when you start to feel lost, just whisper that name, and it will bring you back to yourself.

HOMEWORK: With reverence, say the name of Jesus twenty times today.

~

REVERENCE IN WORD

The monks should wake up even earlier on Sunday. After the usual prayers, the abbot should read a lesson from the Gospel, while the rest of the community stands in fear and trembling. If—God forbid—the brethren wake up late, some of the lessons or the responses may have to be shortened. When this happens, the monk at fault should make a public apology in the chapel.

—Chapter 11: Morning Prayer on Sundays

Saint Benedict foresees only one occasion when the monks should cut short Sunday prayers: when, by some accident, they fail to wake up on time. And whoever is at fault needs to make an apology to everyone, including God. Prayer, you see, is fundamentally an act of justice. We *owe* God our prayer. It's not something we do for ourselves (though we gain much from prayer), and it certainly isn't a favor we do for God (though of course it pleases Him). When we neglect our prayers, we are actually cheating God out of something that is His due.

Truly each of us has a right to a personal encounter with Jesus, but so too He has a right to a personal encounter with each of us. And the priv-

ileged time and place for that encounter is Sunday at church, because when we pray *together* in Christ, we are no longer strangers, but "fellow citizens with the saints and members of the household of God, built upon the foundation of the apostles and prophets, Christ Jesus himself being the capstone" (Eph 2:19–20).

When Saint Benedict reflects on how his monks should say their Sunday prayers, therefore, he uses this unusual phrase: *cum honore et tremore*—"with honor and trembling". Benedict wants his monks to feel the importance of the Sabbath. Sure, we are obliged to be there, but more importantly, we are privileged to be there. We are honored to be there, and we tremble at the magnitude of that honor. Of course, that's hard to do when we are sleepy or the music stinks or the congregation is obnoxious and lukewarm. At times like these, we must try to see with the eyes of faith. This, ultimately, is what we mean by *custodia oculorum*.

HOMEWORK: This Sunday, set an alarm to go off every thirty minutes. Whenever the alarm sounds, stop what you are doing and say an Our Father.

REVERENCE IN DEED

Nothing should be preferred to the Work of God.
If a monk should arrive late for prayer, he should
not stand in his usual place, but should take the
lowest rank in choir. This way, perhaps he will
be shamed into changing his behavior.

—Chapter 43: Tardiness

f all the passages in the *Rule*, this one makes me the most uncomfortable. I'm so consistently late for everything, my own brother monks have started calling me "the late Brother Augustine". Truly this is one area where I have no authority to preach. But in good conscience, I can't skip it either, so I'll just have to play the hypocrite.

The monk may have other things to do in the course of the day, but prayer is the Work of God (*Opus Dei*, in Latin). So properly speaking, prayer is the monk's job. Other religious orders have other jobs. Franciscans work with the poor, Dominicans preach, Jesuits teach, Christian Brothers run schools, and so on; but the work of the monk is uniquely simple: he prays. That's it. Anything else he does is simply to support, enhance, or enable this prayer. And in many respects, that should be a

rule for everyone. Holiness must be the first priority in your life, because who cares how hard you work if, at the end of the day, you are still the same lousy person you were when you started?

Like any other form of employment, prayer has to be done consistently. If you want to keep your job and show your boss that you take it seriously, you have to show up every day and punch the clock. Saint Benedict would add that you also show what your priorities are by being there on time. (Imagine me now fiddling with my beads and not looking you in the eye while I say this.) You show up early so that you can prepare yourself for prayer. You show up early so that you can do the job right. But most of all, you show up early because it shows God —and everyone else—that Jesus is the first priority in your life. When the bell rings for prayer, the monk drops whatever he's doing because absolutely nothing is preferred to the Work of God.

HOMEWORK: Arrive twenty minutes early for church this Sunday.

~

CONCLUSION

The purpose of this Rule is to help you to be holy —or at least to help you get started. So do your best to fulfill this little rule for beginners; and you will, by the grace of God, reach the heights of knowledge and virtue.

—Chapter 73, The Purpose of the Rule

ack when I first decided to join the monastery, my roommate from college decided to go off to Los Angeles to become a movie star. Randall was on *The Young and the Restless* and made guest appearances on sitcoms. He was in movies and hung out with models and rock stars. One night, I received a call from him on the monastery phone. He said to me "Guess who was just named *Teen* magazine's 'Hunk of the Month'!"

I said to him, "Well, I'm in a monastery, so it must be you."

As you might imagine, Randall's stories started to become a real temptation to me. Whenever life in the monastery seemed dull or lonely, I would think of him. So a few years passed, and after I professed my Solemn Vows, I went to visit him in New York. He had a little party in my honor. All of his beautiful friends were there: models, producers, musicians—and they were all beautiful. The loft was beautiful. Randall and his wife were beautiful. The hors d'oeuvres were beautiful. Even the little toothpicks were beautiful. I was really taken with all this beauty, and having a serious vocation crisis all to myself, when this chic jewelry designer from Soho named Claudette leaned toward me over the coffee table and said, ''Why did you have to become a monk? Isn't it enough just to be a good person?''

She couldn't have picked a worse time to ask. But, as sometimes happens, the Holy Spirit stepped in on my behalf. I slapped my beautiful hors d'oeuvre down on the coffee table and said, ''No! No, it is not enough 'just to be a good person'. That's the least you can do. That's the minimum. Think about it. What's the alternative? You're expected to be a good person. But God wants you and me to be saints—to live lives of heroic virtue —to give and give and give until it hurts!'' Then I stabbed myself with a toothpick and had to run to the bathroom.

My point is that humility should never be confused with mediocrity. Perfect holiness is the purpose for which we were created, so we can't allow ourselves to be comfortable with the status quo. The minimum is not enough.

Does this scare you? It should. ''Everyone to whom much is given, of him much will be required" (Lk 12:48). But it should also thrill you, because it means you are infinitely important and always loved. What's more, you have a whole army of saints at your back. You have volumes and volumes of guidance to draw upon. You have the Sacraments and the Scriptures at your disposal—and all the resources of an exceedingly ancient religion. So get to it. You know the steps, now climb the ladder.

HOMEWORK: Give this book away.

~

ACKNOWLEDGMENTS

o many thanks to my brothers, the monks of Saint Louis Abbey; to my first editors, the brilliant and humble students of the Saint Louis Priory School; to Father Henry Wansbrough and the gentlemen of Saint Benet's Hall, Oxford; to Joanna Weaver for encouraging me when I was still just a wannabe; to Dawn Eden for encouraging me to keep writing; to Rachel, Mary, and Georgia Decker who have devoted so much time and effort to keeping me humble; to Jean and Frank Wetta for teaching me how to fake it; to Father Joe Hill for showing this manuscript to the right people; to Bernie Kilcullen, Dianna Hartnett, Jared Rashford, and Michael Nickolai for their patience; to Nicholas Parafiniuk for his patience and wise counsel; to Father Francisco Schulte who was the first monk I ever met; to Abbot Christopher Jameson for the charitably blunt advice; to Father Timothy Horner for founding my monastery and condescending to read this manuscript; to Father Paul Chovanec for teaching me the value of dogged perseverance; to Walter Hooper for being my Oxford granddad; to Lola and August Brown for their hospitality; to Judy Merrill Larsen for the sage advice; to the Henneberrys, the Owens, and the Nassars for their prayers; to Cardinal Burke and Bishop Braxton for leading with courage; to the Kwai Nyu Rugby Club, without whom this book would have been written much sooner; to Detective Veronica Jadzinski for her brave and meticulous work; to Father Ambrose Bennett and Mr. Tom Carroll for helping me translate Saint Symeon's poem; to the gracious souls of the Antioch Writers Workshop; to Vicki Hudson for bringing me to the San Francisco Writers Workshop, where I met Eric Larsen and a couple hundred more allies in the War on Despair; lastly, a loud thanks to Sister Pita for the regular dose of reality.

∽

ILLUSTRATION SOURCES

All of the illustrations inside this book were created by the author using art found on the internet. These sources are listed below by page number, and most of them are in the public domain.

8 Master of the Geneva Boccaccio. *Travaux des douze mois de l'année*. College Sainte-Barbe, France. Wikimedia Commons.

10 Filippo Balbi. *Painted Door with [Carthusian] Monk and Cat (Fra Fercoldo nel chiostro della certosa di S. Maria degli Angeli)*. Livioandronico2013. Wikimedia Commons.

Wetta, Jean C. *Polo*.

(These images also appear on 26, 38, 50, 62, 74, 86, 98, 110, 122, 134, 146, 158, 170.)

13 *Benedikt von Nursia*. Gerd A.T. Müller. Wikimedia Commons.

16 *Cours de philosophie à Paris Grandes chroniques de France*. Bibliothèque Municipal, Castres, France. Vol de nuit. Wikimedia Commons.

18 Piero della Francesca. *Madonna della Misericordia*. Mes images d'Italie. Dmitry Rozhkov. Wikimedia Commons.

25 The Olivetan Master (Girolamo da Milano) and the Master of the Lodi Choir Books. Detail *Monks Singing the Office*. Courtesy of Sam Fogg, London.

28 *Marginal Painting of a Friar with a Musical Instrument and a Woman Dancing from the Maastricht Hours.* British Library.

30 Matthew Paris. *The Monk Matthew Paris on His Deathbed.* British Library Catalogue of Illuminated Manuscripts.

33 Bartolomeo di Giovanni. *S. Benedetto benedice vino avvelenato.* Sailko. Wikimedia Commons.

36 Hildebert and Everwin. *Hildebert Cursing a Mouse.* Moravia Magna. Wikipedia. Ofirka991. *Drums.* Wikimedia Commons.

40 Raymund of Peñafort. *Monk Driving Off a Devil.* British Library Catalogue of Illuminated Manuscripts.

42 Paul Brennan. *Classic Car Parked on Street.* Public Domain Pictures.

Miller, David C. *Paradise.* Pixabay.

Aretino, Spinello. *Fondazione di Montecassino e miracolo del frate risorto.* Sailko. Wikimedia Commons.

45 Pittore Lombardo. *Ritratto di un frate francescano.* Accademia Carrara, Bergamo, Italy. Used with permission.

Tom Young and David Lewis, *Plan 9 from Outer Space.* Internet Movie Poster Awards, Wikimedia Commons.

48 Eduard von Grützner. *In der Studierstube.* Dorotheum. Wikimedia Commons.

Eduard von Grützner. *In der Klosterküche.* Dorotheum. Wikimedia Commons.

52 Piero della Francesca. *Augustinian Monk.* aiwaz.net. Wikimedia Commons.

54 Bill Ebbesen. *Arctic Monkeys - Orange Stage - Roskilde Festival 2014.* Wikimedia Commons.

Francesco Guarino. *St Anthony Abbot and the Centaur.* Web Gallery of Art.

57 Juan Rizi. *La cena de San Benito.* Museo del Prado, Madrid. Wikimedia Commons.

60 *Benedictine Monks Chanting.* British Library Catalogue of Illuminated Manuscripts (39636, ff. 10, 13, 28, 29f. 10).

64 Lucca di Tomme. *Virgin and Child with Saints.* Web Gallery of Art. Wikimedia Commons.

66 Ludovico Mazzanti. *San Giuseppe da Copertino si eleva in volo alla vista della Basilica di Loreto.* Turismo Si. Wikimedia Commons.

Amila Tennakoon. *Surfing Sri Lanka.* Flickr.

69 Grützner, Eduard von. *Beschauliche Ruhe.* Dorotheum. Wikimedia Commons.

72 Luca di Tommè. *Virgin and Child with Saints.* Web Gallery of Art. Wikimedia Commons.

Md-2. *Water Skiing.* Flickr.

76 *Initial C: Monks Singing.* J. Paul Getty Museum, Los Angeles.

78 *Cistercian Monks at Work.* Paradoxplace. Wikimedia Commons.

81 Bartolomeo di Giovanni. *San Benedetto salva San Placido.* Sailko. Wikimedia Commons.

84 Jacopo de' Barbari. *Portrait of Fra Luca Pacioli and an Unknown Young Man.* Web Gallery of Art. Wikimedia Commons.

88 Petrus Christus. *Portrait d'un Chartreux*. Metropolitan Museum of Art, New York. Wikipedia.

90 Ludolph of Saxony. *Monk Writing a Manuscript*. Used by permission of University of Glasgow Library, Special Collections.

93 Monaco, Lorenzo. *Benedikt Erweckt den Kleinen Klosterbruder zum Leben*. Yorck Project. Wikimedia Commons.

96 *Initial D: A Monk with His Finger to His Lips*. J. Paul Getty Museum, Los Angeles.

100 Fra Filippo Lippi. *Saints Augustine and Francis, a Bishop Saint, and Saint Benedict*. The Metropolitan Museum of Art, New York.

102 Andrew Katsis. *A Climber Boulders a Cliff-face at Hanging Rock, Australia*. Wikimedia Commons.

Brother Rufillus, *Illuminating the Initial R*. Foundation Martin Bodmer, Cologny, Switzerland. E-Codices. Wikimedia Commons.

105 Jörg Breu the Elder, *Cistercians at Work*. Yorck Project. Wikimedia Commons.

DualD FlipFlop. *Flying High*. Flickr.

108 Fra Angelico. *St. Anthony the Abbot Tempted by a Lump of Gold*. Web Gallery of Art.

112 Paul Mercuri. *Medieval Priest, Friar, or Monk*. Old Book Art. Wikimedia Commons.

114 Signorelli Sodoma. *Come benedetto perdona al monaco che volendo fuggire del monastero trova uno serpente nella via*. Vignaccia76. Wikimedia Commons.

117 Fra Angelico. *Apparition of St. Francis at Arles*. Web Gallery of Art. Wikimedia Commons.

Craig Howell. *Belly Flop Aftermath*. Flickr.

120 Giovanni Bellini. *St. Francis in Ecstasy* (*St. Francis in the Desert*). Google Art Project. Wikipedia.

Ben Stanfield. *Hang On*. Flickr.

124 Niccolo di Ser Sozzo. *Virgin and Child with Saints*. Web Gallery of Art.

126 Fra Angelico. *Saint Romuald*. Yorck Project. Wikimedia Commons.

129 *Monk Drinking from Barrel*. British Library. Flickr.

132 *Miniature of Monks Seated in a Choir*. British Library Medieval Manuscripts Blog.

Big Dipper. Pixabay.

136 Details from an Illuminated Manuscript. British Library Catalogue of Illuminated Manuscripts.

Jean Pichore. *Book of Hours*. Walters Art Museum, Baltimore.

138 Hieronymus Bosch. *Anthony with Monsters*. Yorck Project. Wikimedia Commons.

141 Details from *Gorleston Psalter*. British Library Digitized Manuscripts.

144 Eduard von Grützner. *Brotzeit*. Dorotheum. Wikimedia Commons.

148 *Egbert Psalter*. Yorck Project. Wikimedia Commons.

150 *St. Benedict Delivering His Rule to the St. Maurus and Other Monks of His Order*. Monastery of St. Gilles, Nimes, France. Wikimedia Commons.

NOTES

NOTES